1982

Living
With
Everyday Problems

by
EUGENE KENNEDY

THOMAS
MORE
PRESS

ISBN: 0–88347–036–5

F. S.

Contents

CHAPTER ONE

A Movable Feast

"If I can just get through this problem, then everything will be all right." This may be one of the most common of English sentences, a tribute to human optimism and a footnote to almost any season of an individual's life. There comes a time—and it may be the birth of maturity—when we suddenly realize that if we do get through our present problem, there will be another one, slightly larger and a little more intense, waiting to take its place. That time when "everything will be all right" recedes a little further into the distance, the light in the sky above it grows dim, and men and women finally forget it altogether. It is like never-never land for the average, hard-working adult. He or she likes to dream about it, of course, and perhaps even buy a few acres in the mountains or in the painted desert where, free of burdens at last, they will settle into a content retirement. The fact that fewer than 10% of the people who purchase hide-a-way land ever build anything on it—and some never even lay eyes on it—attests to the elusive quality of that earthly Eden where problems will be no more. In truth, life seems like a long unbroken line of challenges, swarming before us like knowing pan-handlers who will not be shaken off a sure thing.

Most of the problems that wait for us are homely and familiar if still uncomfortable to deal with or to acknowledge. It is not, in other words, the dramatic life that is crowded with difficulties. You don't have to have Romanoff bad luck or be born under a surly star in order to discover your share of difficulties. That is why soap operas and true confession magazines have such a large and undiscourageable audience; these phenomena take people a little bit away from themselves and their own life situations. The vicarious identification with noble heroines and misunderstood heroes eases the burden of getting through each day. The playlets and magazines add drama to the tedious long pull of the ordinary person's existence. The central characters are handsome, the conflict is sharply etched and they provide something that a person can really cry or get enraged about. These entertainments help a person get out from under the often nameless, routinely dull, and mostly insoluble difficulties that mark the adult years. Life, for most people, comes wrapped in plain, brown paper but the contents are far from anything racy or exciting; they are more like that vexing joke of boxes tucked in other boxes and there is no end to opening them.

This is not to say that life is impossible; it is, however, to observe that it is steadily difficult and that we need to see it in proper perspective if we are going to understand it or bring our human resources successfully to bear on it. It helps to realize that our difficulties in life are not totally separate from us nor need they be classed as enemies; they are the signs that we are alive, that we have become engaged in life enough to feel its strain in our bones. Life does not consist of solving problems and then setting them aside the way an engineer does with the progressive difficulties of building a bridge; we never really put an important problem of living completely aside. Life consists of our continuing response to the constantly shifting weather conditions of our existence. It is a process which has its highs and lows but in which we are always a central organizing presence; it is a movable feast that changes its moods but never sums itself up completely.

LIVING WITH
EVERYDAY PROBLEMS

We are in the middle of a process when we are invested in living and our problems, rising like ghosts outside our windows, are aspects of our dynamic effort to understand and become and share our meanings with others. Our problems—the everydays ones—are us; they spring from our imperfect human staging and they follow us, ballooning out here and flattening there, through our days. The essential problem is that we are human; it is a difficulty we cannot shake off and that we surely cannot solve. The more we enter into life, the more clearly, and sometimes painfully, we feel the pebbly cloth of the human fabric. The things which we call individual problems are inevitable aspects of being human; they are the scenery that goes with the journey Sometimes it is challenging and at other times it is refreshing; if we did not have it we would have no idea of the conditions or meaning of our pilgrimage.

Wisdom and peace come with the recognition that being alive is a process rather than a set of separate exercises or problems; there are, then, continuing problems that are sown into the very idea of being either a man or a woman. These are clearly not settled merely by being born male or female; to be a person is a task to be carried out, one that causes us to search ourselves into old age for the deep truths of our identity. Our unique personality is something, after all, which we are constantly refining and deepening. Unless we cop out in some way, the challenge to bring more of ourselves into life is the healthiest kind of problem we can have. It looks different at different ages—a boy learns to be a friend and then to be a husband and a father and it is not ended then —and each stage has a cluster of challenges that demand something more of him that is clean and true. We go through life mining our own resources, building new dimensions of ourselves on the structures we have just laid down. The everyday problems come in connection with growing. These are always invitations to develop and to come to grips with the difficulties that arise in each new moment. We don't really get through life by solving problems in a final way but by responding more adequately as we move along.

Everyday problems reveal man as quite vulnerable and yet at the same time as quite strong. In fact, the person never feels his own human strengths until he must bring them to bear in some situation in which he experiences the tension of challenge. A man may never know what is inside himself unless, for example, he falls in love. Many people describe friendship

and love as two of the human situation's more serious problems. There are advice books enough to fill
a modest library on how to win friends, lovers, or
even husbands or wives. Manipulation and trickery,
however, are not the responses of choice for the
individual who finds himself face to face with love.
Everybody knows that love has its stages, everybody, that is, but the person who is in love. He or
she will get lots of advice on how to impress the
other or, perhaps, make the other jealous or whatever else seems desirable at the moment. In the long
run, however, and after all the tricks are played out,
the individual has his or her honest self to make
present to the other person.

The problem is not solved by making an impression or coaxing affection out of another; those things
are usually parts of the problem. The person can
only live his way into a truer and better solution;
love asks people to become more of their true selves
in each other's presence, and to become more
steadily alive and sensitive to each other's person. If
love is a problem, there is no easy solution, certainly
not one that can be coached in from the sidelines.
Persons who love each other discover that they have
a new claim on their being, a new sense of themselves, and a thousand lessons to learn. Growing into

a deeper love is not a problem but the necessary condition for an enriched existence. Because they are in love a couple feel life more keenly and they must commit themselves to constant self-revision and change; through their love they make purchase of the experiences that make us human.

Love, in other words, involves people in the process of living and everyday problems are a healthy consequence of this. Lovers become different people together over a lifetime; it is everything they meet along the way—and most of it centers on responding more fully in a variety of human relationships—to which we give the name life itself. There is no safe and easy path along its rim; the harvest of challenging situations that ranges from raising children to taking care of aging parents flows from that moment when, without quite knowing what we are doing, we break into life itself. We must learn to live with our everyday problems, not as cruel injustices that must be stamped out or overcome, but as the human substance of purposeful existence. We never have these real problems when we stay on the surface of life; there is no need to resent them when they come. They are meaningful signals that should reassure rather than distress us; our problems are just the changing face of our human situation

LIVING WITH
EVERYDAY PROBLEMS

It is better, in other words, to find yourself worried about another human being than to be upset because the clock in your Rolls Royce is a few minutes slow. That latter difficulty looms large only in the environment of an individual who has not heard the news about life yet. The difficulties of the transforming human condition make us come face to face with things that count. We may fall short of being everything we would like to be in response to some of these and yet that is not the crucial issue. It is better to have attempted to respond well as a human being and to have made some mistakes in the process than it is to stay completely aloof from the complicated business of life. There are no problems that can be separated from ourselves and there are no solutions that are perfect and lasting. Loving is a long-term challenge, just as staying in relationship to one's children is. The problems that crowd the way, from broken promises to broken arms, are incidental to the more basic process of being alive to others.

Taking life seriously rather than trying to find some cure for it necessarily exposes us to various sized hazards. It can sometimes seem that life is out to break our heart or our spirit; holding on is occasionally about as good a response as we can muster.

That is because persons who move willingly into the depths of life—that is, persons who take themselves and others seriously—feel the vectors of existence in their souls. They deal with the experience of time, for example, and they know it in a way that they could never understand unless they are willing to affirm themselves and each other. Lovers must live in and with time, sensing that it passes but also learning that what they feel for each other challenges and finally triumphs over it. They face the pain of separation and know that love closes all distances. They deal with what it means to be true to each other and to themselves and richer insight comes because each step forward asks more of them. Their life is filled with what we might term problems but they are signs that things are going right rather than that everything is going wrong.

It is not easy for persons to be philosophical about their burden of difficulties. If, however, they could invest a fraction of the energy and ingenuity which they sometimes use to avoid problems to face them calmly and honestly, they would earn mature dividends. There is a two-fold penalty in the refusal to face life as it is. We fool ourselves when we deny or rationalize our shortcomings—as, for example, in friendship or love when we are so easily inclined to place blame or burden on the other person—in order to make ourselves seem virtuous or at least blameless. First of all, we fool only ourselves and do not change the situation in reality by as much as a millimeter. Secondly, we complicate but do not free ourselves from the problem by denying or mislabeling it. There are some people who use the same technique with life's challenges that Napoleon supposedly used with his mail. They ignore them, presuming that they will somehow solve themselves before they have to exert any energy in their regard. That may be the style, for example, of the cool person, who affects a studied detachment to avoid snaring his feelings on any person or event. Nothing bothers him, he tells us, and so his heart seems free of the storms that break inside our own. He may travel a long way through life by keeping others at bay emotionally. But is he, in fact, alive? And what, in the long run, does he save of himself? He may keep free of incidental difficulties but only because he has left a large hole in the center of his existence. There is a price involved in looking away from problems or in so leading our lives that we do not let them bother us. The person who lives in this manner may congratulate himself, as billionaire J. Paul Getty once did, by saying he never let anyone get close to him. Isolation, numbness, terminal loneliness; these are the incurable problems that come to those who stay outside life and its everyday problems. They never even realize that it is a feast and a marvelously movable one at that.

What we believe is crucial to our manner of making our way through life. Lacking a philosophical or theological perspective an individual may have limited alternatives in dealing with the common, garden-variety problems of living. He or she may only have the far reaches of escape or the troubled avenues of madness to pursue in search of a solution. Most persons, however, do have a way of looking at life which, even if it is not sophisticated, may reflect enough of their religious traditions to support their days with a sense of meaning. The role of religion in supplying a context of significance for our ordinary difficulties is still of fundamental importance. The universe must be made believable through the religious systems of interpretation and symbolization that can touch even the unlettered. In other words, there is a special language of faith that is very removed from the abstract reasoning of the theological *aula*. It is the faith language of experience that speaks of the everyday resonations of trying to live honorably and lovingly with appreciation and sensitivity. This language of faith permits us to translate our own first hand grapplings with existence into a tongue that makes their deeper meanings available to us. The Sacraments and the Liturgy are not entertainment, dutiful worship exercises, or sentimental rituals; they give us a perspective on our own meaning in terms of the teachings of Jesus that we could not otherwise know. Religion, then, is an indispensable resource for the ordinary man and it is precisely because it is so extraordinarily relevant to everyday life that its renewal and adequate proclamation are important.

Living with everyday problems demands a readiness to vote in favor of life and of the pains and joys that go with it. It involves an acceptance of ourselves as we are and a willigness to grow into the best version of our personality that is possible. The values that are lasting will be tapped in our passage through life: the question of whether we can believe or hope or touch people with love. These will, in a very real sense, provide the center of gravity and the strength that we need in order to make our journey by the route that is best for us. The trip becomes increasingly joyful as we give ourselves wholeheartedly to it. The biggest problem is that simple everyday one of being human. We solve it only bit by bit through the process of living itself.

CHAPTER TWO

Living With Yourself

The first thing on our agenda is sometimes the last thing we attend to: coming to terms with our true selves. It involves honesty, openness to pain, and the capacity not only for surprise but for joy as well. Getting to know who we are is not accomplished in an instant; it is more like the kinds of revelations that arise gently out of a long friendship with somebody else. These cannot be forced or manufactured nor are they the products of crash programs in self-development. There is a process quality to the emergence of the self that we must learn to accept and ride with if we are to achieve a lasting sense of ourselves. This does not come cheaply and some of the pains and problems we encounter along the way are actually the indications that we are getting somewhere, the rough edges of the process rubbing against our psyches.

LIVING WITH
EVERYDAY PROBLEMS

One of the greatest difficulties connected with self-knowledge is our inborn conviction that it is going to be painful. This is a misrepresentation which cheats us of this special wonder and deep happiness that go along with finding out who we are. Living the truth of ourselves opens the way to sharing ourselves with others and to the joys of being human that are forever locked off from the fearful and the timid. Matthew Arnold once wrote, "He who finds himself, loses his misery." Facing hard truths about ourselves may be uninviting but it need not generate the desperate feelings that inhabit the soul of a man awaiting his execution. Learning to live with the particular mixture of strength and weakness that constitutes our personality is not just something for which we have to grit our teeth; self-knowledge is not all painful and, when it is balanced by a healthy self-acceptance, we can even learn to live more comfortably with our faults. When we get these into perspective and can take them into account in our activities, we find that we can do better in many situations than we had anticipated when we were overcome with a sense of all that was wrong or depressing about us. It is when we take a good look at our shortcomings that we come closest to our identity and, while we may not be pleased with everything that we see, we are at least in possession of reality. Authentic self-knowledge—living with ourselves as we are—makes it possible for us to live more deeply and with greater gratification with other human beings. When we are blind to what is going on inside of us, our other relationships become complicated problems in themselves which we cannot solve because we lack the key of self-understanding. The Japanese have a proverb that the man who protects himself from the raindrops will never find out how beautiful they are. Learning to live with ourselves is something like that. There will be things we do not like and things we wish to change. But we will also find the truth about ourselves and our God-given possibilities. Far from being enslaved by our weak points we will have a surer sense of our strengths and may bring them to bear more effectively on our lives.

It is unfortunately true that many people feel uncomfortable or uneasy with themselves. They look away from themselves and are glad for those moments that can distract them from themselves. It may be this overlay of basic uneasiness that makes deeper self-knowledge unattractive. Sometimes they do not quite know why they feel ill at ease with themselves and it takes much reflection, and sometimes professional counseling, to help them understand their vague uneasiness about themselves. The feelings are familiar enough, in any case, and include a generalized sense of guilt or of somehow being less worthy or good than other persons. In the same way some people feel uneasy with their bodies, estranged to some degree from them and uncomfortable with some of their human feelings, like anger and sex. Many others feel inhibited in expressing themselves, as though a sense of their own unity always just eludes them, so that they can never present themselves to others as fully as they want. They have difficulty, for example, in giving or receiving affection. These are not massive abnormal situations as much as they are the standard kinds of difficulties with which persons must come to terms if they are going to have happy and productive lives.

It has been said that next to living with oneself the next most difficult task is to live with someone else. Most of our problems—and most of our experiences of self-discovery and growth—are linked to other individuals, to our friends or to those we love, or those close to us in one way or another. The major difficulty in life is that it is such a complicated business to grow up with other people, with mothers and fathers, brothers and sisters, and with the whole range of misunderstandings and distortions which

can so easily creep into even the warmest family
scene. This is a subtle atmosphere where small
events or unspoken attitudes can shape significantly
our way of looking at ourselves and other people.
Even in relatively healthy family settings, the problems are always present. The potential for misunderstanding, unconscious rejection, or paralyzing
at least temporarily the growth of another is always
there. We are person-sensitive and, as we begin to
get a picture of ourselves it is sharply affected by
the way other people look at us and by the way
they really feel about us. The basic questions center not on whether we are accepted as we are but
whether our parents demand that we behave in a
way that is false to our true personality. Some parents take their children on approval as though they
were returnable merchandise; they communicate to
them their conditioned view of the child's worthiness
and it may take many years for the child to understand how much his attitude has become a part of
his own way of looking at himself.

The problem, of course, arises because no family is
perfect and only its sustaining love makes it possible for its members to overcome and deal with the
complicated forces that sometimes seem to set them
against each other. Some people spend their entire

lives trying to figure out what has happened to them in their family life, the ghosts of which ride them to the grave. In the ordinary, reasonably healthy family, however, there is enough insight and forgiveness as well as compensating love to make it possible for each individual to come to a reasonable compromise about his or her identity. There is a process quality to this, of course, but the raw material is there and, to some extent, the growing is up to the individual.

He will have to handle many cultural pressures which would also force a false sense of himself onto his personality. While the churches often receive a great deal of blame for making man feel guilty about the vein of evil that runs through the column of his personality, the charge could be made against other enterprises as well. The American environment also provides a host of possible personal identifications that are, in the long run, shallow and unrewarding. They range from the playboy to the politician or financier. Contemporary America has raised to a fine art the notion of getting through life by looking good. When appearances are exalted—even in questions of governmental honesty where making lies sound like the truth has become a way of life—then it is difficult for people to find the root and ground of themselves. They are led on, always with promises that this is the path to the gold, to end up with a bitter taste in their mouth, deprived of heroes and desolate about the possibility of ever achieving a stable emotional identity.

It is no wonder that people are soothed by a psychological program that allows them to find out that they are okay, that the pieces of themselves can fit together despite the tumbled relationships between the parent, child and adult within them. Perhaps one of the greatest sources of tension for people seeking to understand themselves stems from the recurrent calls to perfectionism which have manifested themselves in a variety of ways, from being the perfectly urbane man about town to the programmed virtue of the mechanical saint. To do the right thing and not to make oneself vulnerable to failure or embarrassment has become a pervasive ethic. Man, of course, systematically falls short in all these endeavors. That is one of the reasons that he can settle for going through life by trying to look good. Appearances have great significance in codes of perfection because they have emphasized external behavior unrealistically. They have made it difficult for individuals to come to terms with what is going on internally, to cover up, to make the right move, to know the right wine to order; these are unsatisfactory substitutes for the spontaneous response that comes from a wholeness within the individual. A superficial perfectionism makes it hard for an individual to understand what it means to be normal, or to accept his own shortcomings, or to become a participant in life's movable feast of growth. Living with yourself means giving up superficial perfectionism for a steadier and deeper life lived from the inside out. Perhaps it could begin with the recognition of normality itself as an imperfect state, as one that is coexistent with symptoms and one that depends finally on the truth rather than fiction or putting a good front on things. A man begins to live easier with himself when he can feel the truth in the saying that it is marvelous and normal to be imperfect.

Being normal can have many meanings, but we choose not to speak of it as a statistical average or a complex of cultural expectations on our behavior. Instead, normal means that which is healthy. Health is something that we can instinctively sense even when we cannot logically explain our response to a situation. Health manifests itself in the differences between people that emerge when they can free themselves from overweighted expectations, cultural distortions, or a failure to forgive themselves for their own shortcomings. Health is encountered in people who are open to life and to each other and who are able to call things inside and outside themselves by the right names and who keep saying yes to the ongoing process of their own development. But health is not perfection or very few of us would be healthy in any sense of the word.

It is healthy to be sick, if we understand the term correctly. There is no physical specimen, no matter how marvelously endowed genetically or finely trained physically, who is completely healthy. Look close enough and there is always a blemish, a scar, a slightly chipped tooth, or a cold in the head. All these things are compatible to feeling and being healthy; shortcomings exist, in one form or another, in human beings when they are at what we call their best. The relative profession of the human condition is not a static and unchanging field; it is a living inner state whose external signs are unmistakable. Any person who is involved in the process of life knows that there will be good days and bad, misunderstandings and mistakes, things to forgive and things for which to seek forgiveness. These are the elements through which we experience and demonstrate our health. We do this with each other and the area of our interpersonal experience may be the most sensitive indi-

31

cator of all about how truly well developed we are as human beings. It is the litmus paper that tells the story of whether we have learned to live well enough with ourselves to be able to live lovingly with other persons. The healthy person, however, is not a packaged entity whose outlines are hard and fast and unchangeable for the rest of life. In fact, the healthy person is not a stranger to doubts, mixed feelings, or the other tremors of the heart which so fill life. He has his quota of problems and symptoms and a review of some of these provides us with an inventory of what we will find when we settle down to live with ourselves.

We live best with ourselves when we can strike a balance between the bracketed extremes of certain psychological tendencies. The point is that a person, even while maintaining his balance, will occasionally experience one or the other of the extremes of human emotional reactivity. For example, the mature adult strikes a balance between dependence and independence that enables him to move along constructively in the process of life. He will experience some of both of these feelings, however, and he should be neither dismayed nor surprised by it. If, on the other hand, he or she finds that these reactions cluster at one of the extremes—excessive dependence or overprotesting independence—then they have received a signal to which they should pay heed. Living comfortably with oneself and with others requires us to play both roles. There are times, for example, when we must take care of others but there are also periods when we must allow others to also take care of us; there are moments in which we lead and moments in which we must respond to the initiative of others. These are healthy challenges; we are not talking about neurotic helplessness or a fierce but psychologically unsound search for independence. Healthy living with ourselves demands a capacity to balance both these tendencies and play both of these roles as genuinely as possible in different circumstances. The healthy is manifested in our capacity to balance these responses in appropriate ways.

The same may be said for the blend we must make between putting order into our lives on the one hand and our capacity to let our categories go when a freer and more creative approach to life is indicated. Only the sternly obsessive person gets so hung up on keeping things in order that he is uncomfortable if he has to depart from this for even an instant. The totally disordered individual has no way of organizing himself, his knowledge, or the meaning of his life. Living effectively with our own personality requires us to balance these tendencies so that we are dominated by neither but have the strength of both available to us when we need them.

Other extremes that require a sense of balance are optimism and pessimism. The individual may, after all, be so naively optimistic about himself in life that he clearly does not understand his own make-up or that of individuals in the world around him. He places himself and them in danger because of this fatal pseudo-innocence. His opposite number, the cynically pessimistic individual, can find no good in any human enterprise; everything is fixed from elections to athletic contests and his willingness to believe in anything good about man is sharply attenuated. It is easy for one tendency or other to take over an individual and we can see both of these forces at work in different aspects of our culture. You are not very comfortable living with yourself by clinging to one of these extremes but the capacity to be hopeful that is tempered by realism is indispensable in the healthy adult.

Our sexual identity, a vital aspect of our living comfortably with ourselves, requires the same blend of competing characteristics. No individual is all man or all woman. The balance of masculine and feminine traits that is appropriate to the well-defined male and the fully developed female is a vulnerable balance rather than a defensive posture. It is impossible for most of us to live comfortably with ourselves if we are still preyed upon by fears about our sexual identity; these destroy our sureness of personality and, because we can grow so defensive about these, hamper our participation in life itself.

The way we learn to relate to authority also reveals characteristics with which we should be familiar if we are going to live freely and self-confidently. The healthy person can accept and live with authority, recognizing the right of other individuals in institutions to possess it and understanding the need for some system of rules and regulations as well as that moral standards must govern any developed culture. If a person senses a need to rebel against authority he is far freer even to question or disagree with it when this seems the correct thing to do in his life. The sense of authority is built on a deepening awareness of our appropriate relationships with other persons; this involves us, in other words, in acknowledging that there are times when we respond to authority and times when we exercise it. When we are uncomfortable around the concept of authority, that is an indication that there is unfinished business in understanding our emotional life to which we should give heed. Similar indications come from our response to moments of competition or cooperation with other persons. If we are threatened or uneasy then it is clear that we have touched a sparking live wire in our emotional life and that we cannot leave it unattended.

The healthy person also achieves a balance between emotional control and emotional expression. He is not so constricted that he can never express what he is really feeling but neither is he so volatile that he is likely to explode childishly at any moment. An inability to sense and express our feelings when these are appropriate may be one of the most uncomfortable experiences that we know. A healthy person does not have to be afraid of his feelings; he can trust them when he has grown to the point of understanding their source and their messages to him. He possesses marvelous freedom that makes living with himself a far more pleasant and joyful experience.

A healthy person also understands how to take risks in life. He strikes a balance, in other words, between a fearful holding back from any occasions and relationships in which he may be hurt and the over-eager, impulsive, and usually premature involvement of himself in situations where he is bound to hurt and be hurt at the same time. He cannot play it safe and live freely and fully at the same time. This capacity to risk may be one of the most significant indications that a person has learned well the lessons of life. It is what healthy people do in life all the time because they know that the penalty for not risking is very high. They are prepared to suffer some losses and some hurt but they also recognize that this is the only way for a true and lasting love.

The major question beneath all these reflections comes down to finding oneself and giving proper form to one's own identity so that then one can at least eliminate the unnecessary suffering of life. It is all very well to talk about striking a balance between these extremes and of not being surprised to find these ambivalent tendencies on so many subjects present in one's life. But what are the steps one uses in order to do this? It is a problem of perception, of seeing things truly and clearly and of giving up any tendency we may have to distort or misidentify our life experience. This is not an easy thing because we can all play tricks with life and most of us favor the interpretations of the events we know which enhance us in one way or another. Life is a shifting scene for each one of us and it takes a steady eye and a gentle honesty to track accurately the complex emotions that we must understand in order to live comfortably with ourselves. Harding LeMay, in his recent autobiography, catches some of the flavor of this when he says "I dream, too, of my father, confessing that I am the favorite of his nine sons; later, at breakfast, meeting my 14-year-old's speculative glance, I wonder. What will he remember? What will he invent to conceal what he does remember? What will I remember ten or twenty years from now, of all this that seems so palpable today?" (*Inside Looking Out, A Personal Memoir*, Harper's Magazine Press, New York, 1971).

We begin the search for a more comfortable understanding and acceptance of ourselves by listening more carefully to what we say and observing more accurately what we do. We are constantly giving ourselves messages, writing our signature across our lives in large and unmistakable letters. The other thing is that we so often miss the messages which we are ourselves sending or so misinterpret them that we fail to grasp their significance. There is nothing accidental in our experience or in our expression of our convictions or our attitudes. Everything that we say and do tells part of our story and if we can listen and read this without becoming excessively self-conscious, we will have taken the first step toward understanding and, hopefully, accepting the person we really are. We are telling ourselves about ourselves all the time and, while we are doing this, we are trying to distract ourselves in the way a man might who plays a piano in a nightclub and delivers a comedy monolog at the same time. It is hard to know where his attention really is.

Sometimes it is helpful to see ourselves offguard, in those moments when we are not trying to make an impression, even on ourselves. We might begin, for example, by viewing ourselves in the background of some activity with which we are associated. If we shift our angle of vision from those around us we will be able to see ourselves when we are not on the center of the stage. It is something like changing the Mercator projection of the world, that flat schoolroom map with which we are so familiar. Whenever we see it, the United States is right in the middle, a result of the nationality of the map-makers. If we move some other continent into prominence we suddenly have a very different view of things. So it is with ourselves and the examination of motives and plans with which we are concerned. This allows us to see ourselves more accurately and without the distortion of self-interest or excessive self-concern which ordinarily affects our view of ourselves. If a person can view himself, for example, as a participant in a meeting which is being run by someone else, he may get a quite refreshing view that will be unavailable if he looked at it only from his original viewpoint.

There are many other ways in which we can get a fresh look at ourselves but the important element, no matter how we choose to do this, is to minimize distortion and denial which can tear personality apart. These are the enemies of living either honestly or comfortably with ourselves. They are, in fact, the techniques we use when we fail to listen to or look at certain parts of our emotional lives. Beneath the things we deny, excuse, or cover up with makeup so that they look better are very important parts of our personality. The fact that we try to obscure them does not make them less operative nor less important for us to understand. A man who is too defensive is already living in an uncomfortable situation with himself; it is like living with a roommate with whom you do not get along. There is not space enough for you and your personality so you must shut out this part of yourself. Unlike the roommate, however, that part of yourself remains with you, shadowing you and motivating you in a hundred different ways. He can never be escaped, so if we are seeking balance and a gentle sensitivity to ourselves, we must turn back in his direction.

A very general rule might be that nothing that goes on inside of us—no matter whether we like it or not—should occur without our admitting it, as clearly as we can, to ourselves. We have to call what's going on inside of ourselves by the right name. That is the basic rule of psychological common sense. It is something like asking ourselves to be as understanding toward our own persons as we would be willing to be toward others. This means that, for the moment at least, we can suspend judgment and overeager interpretation and just listen to what emerges in our emotional lives. This takes time and patience with ourselves as well as a readiness to forgive ourselves for what we are truly experiencing. If we automatically block out our capacity to experience any particular feeling or reaction because we would feel ashamed or guilty, then we have cut ourselves off from our own personalities. If I am feeling angry, for example, but will not admit it, that does not make me less angry nor cover up the reasons that gave birth to my anger in the first place. It merely hides the truth about myself from me; it makes me less accessible to myself and, as a result, less genuinely accessible to others. It makes it harder to live with myself when I won't admit what is really taking place inside myself. It is, in fact, only after we can admit what is taking place in our personalities that we can begin to understand or control them.

When we are open to ourselves in this fashion we are far less demanding that we should act in accord with one extreme or the other. We are immediately capable of bringing a greater balance to our activities. This makes life more comfortable right away. There is the significant and potent side effect that further transforms our lives. If our openness to our own experience is genuine, then others will recognize this and feel more comfortable with us too. There is a reciprocal effect initiated by our own willingness to look into ourselves. As we see more, others can also see more of what is true and are less put off by our defensive bluster. We simply do not need that any more and so we can establish relationships that are true and rewarding with much less effort. The response of others also constitutes a kind of validation of our own self-searching; we are no longer living alone but we have made contact with others and they are not the enemy after all. They are instead the source of our continued self-understanding and development.

Very little of this can proceed, of course, unless

we are willing to accept ourselves as less than per-
fectible, unless, in other words, we admit ourselves
warmly and forgivingly into the human situation.
Life is an imperfect process and the comfort with
which we live with ourselves is not that of drugged
somnolence but that of an ordinary human person
who will still feel discouragement, disappointment,
and the other emotional analogs of the common cold.
What we do discover, however, is the capacity to live
with a redeeming tolerance for our frailty and a
deepened capacity for enjoying life. Living comfortably with ourselves begins in that moment when
we can forgive ourselves for being human.

CHAPTER THREE

Living With Others

A problem does not have a life of its own; it does not hang suspended in time and space waiting for us to collide with it. Problems exist because we exist and mostly because we exist in relationship with each other. It is our reaction, whether to a rainy day, a flat tire, or a moody companion, that shapes the problem. Personal reactions are a major factor and that is why it is so important to be able to recognize and identify our own responses to life properly. Reactions are always a part of the problem because it is in and through them that we experience the sadness, pain, or tension that subjectively define a problem situation for us. Our reactions are part of the problem but, as we understand and integrate them, they become part of the solution. This is particularly true of our everyday problems with each other. Our first lesson in dealing more effectively with these is to broaden our focus so that we always see the problems in the perspective of the person who experiences them. A problem, in other words, is not like a package that we can inspect casually or perhaps deposit on the desk of some counselor. The problem is not just a cranky friend, the aged parent, or the suddenly alienated child; the problem is that we are in relationship—it is as though our nerve supply and blood stream would intermingle—with all these people.

Life with others may well be termed the problem of living. It is, of course, a good problem to have. It is at once the best and worst of the human experiences, the hardest and the easiest, the most everyday of everyday challenges and opportunities. It is together that we finally find and express ourselves and begin to understand where the real treasures of existence lie. It is when we stand close to each other that we also know the region of the heart where the pain can be the deepest. For most of us, our lives with each other are the test of our humanity, the main event through which we know and are known in life. It is also a sign of what we believe in and what life means to us; it is even, in the words of Pope Paul VI, "the acid test" of our relationship with God. If we are to understand the challenges of living with others then we can never leave our-

selves and our own emotional reactions out of the
picture. Nor can we forget the subtle, living quality
of what it means to be a friend, a husband or a wife,
a father or a son. There is nothing more clearly a
process phenomenon than the relationships we spend
our lives working out with each other.

We begin our discussion with some general principles about living with other people and, later on,
we will proceed to more specific areas with appropriate suggestions for handling these. If we remain a
constant factor with our problems, however, our first
inquiry might center on what our basic attitude
toward other people really is. Our real feelings toward others also tell us our real feelings about
ourselves. If I am open and trusting toward others
and can forgive them for their failings, the chances
are that I feel the same way toward myself; if, on
the other hand, I am always fearful about others and
close myself off in their presence, the odds are that I
keep the same kind of stand-off relationship with
myself. If I do not make enough room in my life
for others to be free and be themselves it may be related to the fact that I do not grant these privileges
to myself either. It is also possible that we can spend
a good deal of time trying to categorize other individuals and, through this process, bring them under

some kind of subjective psychological control. If, after all, we can name the type of person we are dealing with—the way an amateur psychologist does overplaying his parlor game—then we feel more competent and at ease. In truth, however, such categorization may be inaccurate and seriously deprive us of the richness of human relationship that we could experience if we were more open and less judgmental in our approach. For most of us, especially in the everyday problems of getting along with each other with which we are here concerned, the approach of understanding is far more appropriate than that of psychological analysis.

Understanding has a few fundamental outlines that should help us to express it more accurately and to incorporate it as an attitude toward both ourselves and others. Understanding is what we are always looking for. Each of us sends messages, like a ham radio operator into the darkness, and we are always waiting for a reply. Has anybody picked up our signal? Do they understand what I am trying to say and will I hear back from them? To be understood is one of the most profound of human experiences because it validates a sense of ourselves in the powerful manner that being received by others always does. There is something almost mystical in the need we have for the simple human response of being understood; without it, we are frustrated and unsure of ourselves, outcasts in an uncomprehending world. If we reflect on how much we look for understanding from others, even when we would not consciously so describe our strategy, we might begin to understand just how much other people look for understanding from ourselves. In order to grasp this we must put aside our own point of view and our own willingness to impose judgments on the outside; we also have to yield up our own right or desire to be understood at least for the moment. We are going to respond to the need to be understood expressed by others.

Secondly, we have to make room for the individuality of other persons. We must, in other words, begin to view them as separate from us rather than as extensions of our personalities or as presences placed in our path for our own use or convenience. It is not easy to respect the individual life of another person. That is because we have so many reasons of our own for wanting them to behave in this way or that and because we are so good at convincing ourselves that what we want for them is really the thing they should want for themselves. This is true of teachers with their pupils, pastors with their parishioners, as well as parents with their children. The quest for a healthy sense of separateness is indispensable for the kind of understanding that serves as well in dealing with our everyday problems. It is surprising, indeed, how much the strain of living is eased, in fact, and how much more understanding other people are in response to us once we can begin to use this approach ourselves. We could also factor out of life almost immediately many of the unnecessary but brutal bruising and mindlessly alienating scrapes that come about purely and simply because individuals either cannot or will not try to understand each other.

At the same time understanding does not ask us merely to absorb passively the feelings of others the way a blotter does the trembling ink of a fresh signature. To understand another person does not mean we give up our voting rights and life or give away our own convictions or principles. Any interpretation of understanding which suggests that this is the case is describing another phenomenon that is full of soft and mushy spots. Understanding is abetted when we are able to give it to others without giving up ourselves; acknowledging the separateness of others is strengthened when we can maintain the separateness of ourselves. The more we understand and possess our own feelings, the more surely we can present ourselves with confident understanding in the lives of others. Only a bad distortion of understanding transforms us into sponges; only a misunderstanding of life processes makes us thoroughly unconcerned and passive in the face of others and their struggles. We must retain our own values and convictions as well as our right to express them when this is appropriate. This need not conflict with being understanding and, in the ordinary way of life, this is exactly the way understanding people operate. We are talking about understanding as it is observed between people from day to day and not in the highly specific settings of counseling or psychotherapy. While these may give us a rich insight into understanding and a very sharp and intense picture of it, understanding in everyday life is a more generalized attitude that is powerfully important and influential in our efforts to live lovingly and respectfully with each other.

What do we try to understand? To begin with, the feelings of other persons rather than with their words. Their words, or in some cases, their symbolic gestures, are the ways in which people try to explain their feelings to those around them. All of us are engaged in this most of the time but, for complicated reasons, we frequently stick to the surface and fail to catch the emotional content within our communications which really signs them with meaning. The same sentence after all, even if it is as simple as "Good morning" can have many meanings depending on the feelings with which it is expressed. It may be spoken sarcastically, warmly, or with neutral indifference. If we are too literal, that is, too attached just to the words others speak, we will never hear what they are trying to say. We attempt to keep the total person of the other in our viewpoint rather than just some portion of the other. As we would not overfocus on an individual's problem as though it existed separately from him, so neither can we focus just on his words or we will miss them completely. Quite often, other persons do not know exactly what they are trying to say when they speak to us; they are experimenting in a sense with an effort to define their own meanings while sharing it with us. That is why understanding demands a sensitivity to the lattice beneath that which is strictly literal. Perhaps we can ask ourselves often the following simple question: What is this other person feeling in order to be telling me this story? Behind the answer to that question will come our understanding of the other.

There are many other helpful questions that can

enlarge our practical understanding. One that can
lead to significant insights may be put this way:
What is this other person doing to me in this relationship? Sometimes the real message, or an en-
larged sense of it, comes from the totally nonverbal
area, that is, not at all from what the other says, but
very much from what he or she does. You may have
to feel your way into understanding this and yet it is
vital for survival and human communication. For
example, when a young man comes home and an-
nounces to his parents that he is no longer going to
church, one might prematurely classify this as a
declaration of atheism. If we ask the question that
we have just suggested, we might begin to honor
a deeper and more important meaning. What does a
son do to his parents by such a declaration? He up-
sets them, throws them off balance, or perhaps makes
them angry. The disruptive symbolic significance
of the declaration may help us to understand it as
a young man's way of trying to state his own independence. It may not be the best way but, then,
he may not be able to describe very accurately the
many symbolic ways in which his parents over-
protect or keep him in a dependent role. As we look
more deeply into the situation, we come to see how
untheological the declaration is and how inappro-

priate rational arguments or sending the young man to the local priest or minister would be. The message has to do with the relationship of the parents and the son. An understanding in genuine communication can come only if the individuals involved make the effort and take the time to look deep inside the situation.

A collateral question, in these circumstances, becomes: What am I doing to the other in this relationship? Sometimes, when we are having a difficulty that we cannot quite name, new understanding is delivered with the answer to this question. It also may reveal a pattern or style of relationship which we use on many people, including ourselves. For example, an individual may find that in a certain situation the tension he experiences with another is generated from the fact that he is always trying to beat the other no matter what they are involved in. The individual, in other words, constructs, for whatever reasons, an imaginary competition in his human relationships so that other people become adversaries who must be downed in order to preserve his own self-esteem. An individual may blame many things around him for his difficulties in life until he can answer the question which has just been suggested. Then he may find the beginning of wisdom about himself as well as the opportunity for constructive personality change. The analysis of these transactions and the discovery of the kind of games which we play with each other underlie the success of the work of Dr. Eric Berney and Dr. Thomas Harris. These men have provided individuals with a vocabulary and a framework for answering just such questions about snarled human relationships.

Perhaps we can sum up some of these principles involved in dealing with others in this way. If you want to solve the everyday problems of living, emphasize understanding rather than evaluation. It is very easy, and frequently quite self-gratifying, to sit in judgment on others. This passion of evaluation, however, frequently obliterates even the possibility of seeing another as separate and distinct from us. To be evaluative is almost second nature to many persons, however, and they are genuinely surprised when they examine their attitudes toward others and find how much they do try to categorize or otherwise put in boxes those people around them. Every step at overevaluating others makes it more difficult to achieve the understanding stance which feels compelled neither to agree nor to disagree, neither to find guilty nor to find innocent the other person.

In teaching psychotherapy, I have found a few

simple principles which, although they are given in shorthand fashion, seem essential for individuals who want to work effectively with troubled individuals. These same learnings are helpful to all of us in our everyday problems; although we are not trying to be psychotherapists with our family and friends, there is nothing against our being therapeutic with them. These are not rigid formulas but rather some common sense notions that help us to keep our perspective in straightening out relationships that have become snarled or in bringing light where a temporary darkness has fallen.

The first of these simple rules suggests that we listen to the other carefully and actively on a principle that has always proved out. Other persons, as long as they are willing to talk, try to be helpful. They tell us what is wrong with them, in everyday life, what is bothering them; they try to share their dreams or their longings with us. They do this all the time in a variety of vocabularies. The problem does not often rest in the fact that others are not telling us about themselves as much as it does in the fact that we do not listen or hear what they are saying. The obstacles to this lie frequently within ourselves, as, for example, a tendency to evaluate or impose an interpretation from our own point of view. Once we can stop interfering with what others are trying to tell us, we cannot only hear them more accurately, we can also be in a better and more significant relationship with them. There are no tricks involved in this but it may take a little reflection and some resetting of our own attitude so that it becomes more open and less judgmental. If we stop thinking that we know what other people are going to say, we may begin to hear what they actually are telling us. They are, in fact, quite patient with us and why we do not take them more seriously is a strange mystery. Has anybody ever said to you, "Well, that's what I've been trying to tell you all these weeks" or have you ever heard yourself say, "I know I've heard you say that before but I never understood it until now." You may get the idea.

For example, a college student of my acquaintance has been trying to transfer to another school for over a year. His parents, in quite a literal sense, will not hear of it; that is, although he keeps telling them this, they resist hearing what he is saying. The most I have been able to hear so far is that he is debating the problem—which is not the case at all. In his mind the situation is settled and, in a patient but persistent fashion, he keeps representing his case to them in telephone calls and letters. The reason his parents cannot hear is because they really do not want him to change and so they impose a meaning on his words that is nowhere to be found. They experience anguish but some of it comes from the fact that they simply are not listening to what their son says. The mother begins a typical telephone conversation, for example, by asking: "Well, have you made your mind up yet?" This kind of response, which might fall into the wishful thinking category, is typical in those situations in which people, for reasons of their own, actively fail to listen. The problems that ensue only get more complicated. It is not a bad first principle and an individual is amazed but pleased when he finds that active listening is such a major step toward resolving what seem to be very sticky difficulties.

The second principle is simple enough: don't try to do good. This is meant, of course, in the sense that one should not be a do-gooder. These individuals, whose reputation is notorious, probably do more harm than any other single class of persons we know. By suggesting that people do not do good they are merely pointing out the dangers, even in everyday problems, that surround any deliberate effort to shift this scenery to another person's life. Most do-gooders fail because they neither hear nor understand what is taking place in the relationships in their lives and because they have an obsessive sense that everything depends on them. Psychology speaks of certain individuals who suffer from "rescue fantasies," people who set out to do good in the lives of others. They are responding to a fantasy of themselves in the role of a savior; they are meeting their own needs rather than those of others and, in general, they are part of the problem rather than of the solution.

Most of the real good that is done in the world is done unself-consciously and unobtrusively by persons who respect and respond to others for their sake rather than for some other motive or some grand plan of do-goodism which they have designed themselves. Frequently, these people who try to do good in settling the problems of others end up doing long-term harm. Such, for example, is the case of the priest who, with what he described as the best intentions in the world, constantly covered up for his superior, a diocesan official with a serious drinking problem. The younger priest was out to "do good." No sacrifice was too much, no trip too long to take in order to cover the other man's problem and to allow him to maintain face in public. The tragedy of this style of doing good is that now, in much later years, the older priest has been disgraced because his past has caught up with him. No one now protects him from the personal inadequacies with which he never had to deal himself as long as someone else was protecting him. He is, as he approaches his seventieth year, a nearly ruined man. Part of the problem that is now so difficult to solve came from the fact that for years his friend did so much short-term good in his behalf.

A third suggestion is also deceptively simple: do not try to do well. This gets at the tendency that some people have of treating others as problems to be solved, tasks for which some gold medal or celestial checkmark will be made. Unfortunately, some individuals try to solve everyday problems in a way that will enhance their own self-image. They like the idea of being a successful helper and so, with great self-consciousness at every step, they proceed as though under the watchful eye of a teacher whose approval they want very much. Trying to do things well places an individual on a stage and the way he performs becomes more important than the feelings or the concerns of the other person. Trying to do well takes us out of relationship with others, exaggerating our role and making us state our responses so that they sound good even when they may not be spontaneously appropriate and may not meet the needs or realities of the situation itself. Doing well leads people to view each other as objects in relation to which we exercise a technique that is more important than they are. I recall a friend of mine expressing the feeling perfectly to another acquaintance in this way: "You always make me feel as though I were the subject of your good resolution for the day." This approach to other persons complicates rather than helps in the everyday difficulties of life. Trying to do good and trying to do well are, in fact, two factors that interfere markedly with a clear human communication that ultimately proves to be our best response in the challenge of living successfully with others.

CHAPTER FOUR

Living With Your Family

Despite the well-publicized lingering death of family life in the United States, most of the hard facts and figures seem to demonstrate that it retains astounding vigor. That it is under stress there is no doubt, but much of this arises from the widespread human search for a successful family life. People want both marriage and the family to work so that these experiences respond to and allow them to express their profound needs for healthy closeness, for that intimacy through which we recognize ourselves as human beings. The spiralling cracks in the columns of family life come more from the demands made on it rather than from any liberated assaults on it as a lifestyle. For all the talk about it—and despite all the journalistic eulogies that have been intoned over it—the family remains the essential primary unit of our civilization. Of all the institutions we know, the family, heaving and buckling from internal pressures, is still the only one in which human beings thrive.

Learning to live with your family begins with a realistic view of its possibilities and its problems. Most American families fall somewhere in the middle of the continuum between the fictitious Waltons and the all too real Louds. It helps a great deal if we are not romantically overidealistic on the one hand and not jadedly cynical on the other; family life can and does work but only in the unself-conscious hands of those who understand that it is a continually changing and less than perfect experience. The family setting is rich and real when it matches the nature of the human person, when it creates the conditions in which imperfect but dynamic human beings can grow together. In other words, the family is a living entity that is not a stranger to false starts and mistakes and whose real strengths derive from values that make up for but do not eliminate its shortcomings. The family is, first and foremost, a human enterprise rather than a scientific experiment.

It is in and through our families that we become human persons. This is an important overview for those reflecting on the steady challenges of family life. It is, after all, a tale never fully told, a process that is never frozen in time or space, a reality which depends for its vigor on our undefended commitment and participation. The family provides the experiences of trust, acceptance, and understanding as well as the interpretations of our interactions with life which are fundamental for our personal identity. It also provides us with a sense of our limitations and our first sense of the separateness and rights of other persons. The family breaks us in for life as a man or a woman and the attitude and sense of self we derive from it become crucial and frequently strongly determinative of the rest of our lives. The Christian need not sentimentalize his view of the family to realize that it also shapes his religious sense, not only because it builds the first ideas of faith but also because it is the setting for our experience of incarnation, for taking on the flesh of our own identity and the responsibility for our own lives. In the family we incorporate that fundamental sense of ourselves and others that provides the language and relational experiences that enable us, howsoever poorly, to think of and speak about God. There is a sacred quality to family life because through it we grasp the essential values and experiences that Jesus' teachings underline as the core of redemptive living. Religion does not take us away from the humanity which develops in the heart of the family; it allows us to see deeply into it and to comprehend and celebrate its intrinsically religious nature.

The family is always on pilgrimage, not to distant shrines, but toward the heart of the mystery of growing which is primary in any appreciation of or commitment to a religious understanding of life. The best of theological symbols and worship experiences build on the richness of the human exchanges of faith, hope, and love, which are fundamental to family life. It is in the family that we learn the things about ourselves and others that enable us to conceptualize God and to bring to his service a reasonably well developed sense of ourselves. What we learn in the family enables us to hear, recognize and respond to God's revelation to mankind. People need not become stuffily solemn to realize that the family builds the foundations, if they are to be built, for the life of the Spirit.

The difficulty that plagues most people about important things like family life and religion arises from their mistaken sense that these must both be fairly rigid and correct undertakings that are graced more by repression than spontaneity. In fact, however, since both family life and religious experience seem to fit man so well, we learn best about these through healthy expressions of them. In other words, what goes on in a truly loving family tells us more about man and his faith than weighty volumes of abstract notions about these subjects. Growth and change may well be the chief characteristics of the persons who are genuinely alive in their family environments. Join a family and expect to be transformed, sometimes gently and sometimes rudely, throughout all the years of your existence. The essence of the kind of intimacy through which man discovers and makes himself known is in the slowly turning wheel of experience where dying is always followed by rising. It is by no means easy to give oneself over to a dynamic that demands an unequivocal commitment to continuing personal development. That, however, is the first and most significant lesson of living with a family: you are going to change, your spouse is going to change, and, as your children grow, both of you, in different ways, will continue to renew yourselves in relationship to them. Once this dynamic circle is broken or abandoned, a person stops living with his family. He or she may go on living in some fashion within it or just outside it, but the integrating bonds—through which the energies of creation flow—may be permanently shattered.

The remarkable thing about an experience that is

so central to our understanding of God and man is that it is never carried off perfectly. Family life is, in fact, a series of approximations in which nobody ever gets it quite right, not even on the second or third try. Family life is the place where we keep doing our best and where it does not really matter that we constantly fall short of the perfect performance. Perfection simply does not exist in the experiences of belief and hope and love through which we enter into life with each other. What is worth doing is worth doing imperfectly and of nothing is this more true than of the substantial qualities that constitute the heart of family living. That means, of course, that it is perfectly all right for loving people to make mistakes as long as they retain the honesty to admit and the generosity to forgive themselves and others for them. Family life is not exactly chaos but it does not do very well as a boot camp either. The very best things that we know in life are communicated in half-words and symbols; we never get it all said and that is why we keep saying the true things over and over to each other. We need to hear that we are loved and forgiven just as much as we need to express these feelings to others; we even need to hear ourselves saying these things.

In the same way, we must strain to understand each other at each step along the way, to keep vitally in touch, in other words, so that the inevitable hurts and failures are robbed of the power to destroy us. Families don't fall apart; they let themselves be picked apart or fall into ruin because of abridged communication, dried up forgiveness, and untapped love. Family life is not a forced march; in fact, after a while, it is difficult to keep its members in step with each other. What holds it together are the invisible realities of caring and concern for which there are neither substitutes nor alternatives as the members of a loving family make their way like a joyous straggling band through life together.

Parents need not burden themselves with the notion that there can be no give in their relationship with each other or with their children. The most important long-range relationship in any family is, of course, that between the man and woman who are husband and wife as well as mother and father. That must be kept in fresh focus; it must be worked at, or at least thought about seriously, or the marriage relationship can easily become distorted or destroyed. Becoming parents demands a major adjustment from husband and wife, one that enables them to reach out beyond themselves while at the same

69

time they continue to make special room for each other. The models of manhood and womanhood that the children need for their own identification are best revealed in a man and woman who keep in touch with each other in a mature manner. One is tempted to say that if husband and wife treat their own relationship seriously and sensitively they probably will not make many major mistakes in family life. The first lesson about living with your family turns a couple back to the perennial challenge of living with each other as man and wife. The discussions about women's equality are not wholly inimical to this because they open up new areas for development that are dependent for their effectiveness on the informed cooperation of husband and wife. The many movements, such as marriage encounters, aimed at assisting persons to revitalize their marriages are not accidental occurrences or psychological luxuries. These reorient us to the heart of family living and to the concern with which we must steadily view it.

Correlative to this continuing reciprocal affirmation of husband and wife is the need to perceive and respect the individuality of each member of the family. Only through this recognition of differences can the basic health of a family find expression; its members must be allowed, in a sensible way, to be different. The unreasoned insistence on uniformity or on meeting the needs of one or both of the parents not only frustrates the proper development of the children but also lays the groundwork for a great deal of needless conflict across the generation gap. Parents who insist on making all the decisions for their children—and many retain considerable potential and power to do so—are unwittingly creating many problems for themselves. To master the commitment to growing children that balances their coexistent needs for dependence and independence is one of the unending and approximate tasks of living with a family. The parents who stick at it ultimately make their family experience a far happier one for all concerned.

To this end parents need to give their children both understanding and trust. These can be made to sound like soft notions by the caricaturists of human experience who have never understood these things in their own lives. There is, however, nothing permissive or weak about understanding and trust; these are hard qualities to share because they ask so much of our real selves in the process. In other words, these qualities are rooted in real life in which people stand close enough to be able to hurt each other if they make any false moves; understanding and trust are emotional graftings that transfer strength from the grown to the growing. They are difficult to give because they are personally demanding; we must be present and yet respectfully separate from those we understand and trust. These experiences are powerful precisely because they depend on persons really reaching each other in a strong and active manner. There is no place for weakness or for anything that seems like abandoning another to his or her fate. Almost as remarkable as the dynamics of understanding and trust is the fact that a little of either of these goes a long way in making up for our other shortcomings or for mistakes we have made. These values heal and build, allowing us to realize more of our own selves even as we help others to achieve a deeper sense of their own identities.

Children need to be in relationship to parents who are undefensive enough to be real and who, in accord with their own reasonably well achieved identity, can be consistent but not harsh in their management of family life. More harm is done by inconsistency than by almost anything else in the raising of children. It is when the children do not know what to expect from parents that confusion and conflict arise to make living together a swelling burden. Adults are inconsistent, of course, when they do not know themselves well and cannot present a well-defined presence to others. Parents need to consolidate their sense of themselves in order to offer adequate models for identification and development to their children. This is not a matter of choice but of necessity, especially as one considers the long-term effects of parental uncertainty on the later lives and possibilities of their children. It is in the shadow of the mother and father, after all, that the children learn the basic lessons that prepare them for lives of their own. These lessons are difficult to grasp when parents are unsure of them or the depth of their own convictions about them. Living with a growing family necessitates an early coming to terms with ourselves.

Family life may be complicated enough in itself but it is also constantly under siege from a variety of relatives and other interested parties. Living well with one's family demands some attention to the complexities of living with, near, or in relationship to relatives. It may seem sad but it is also wise for a family to build some kind of distance—call it a loving distance if you will—between itself and even the most affectionate of relatives. That, in fact, is the way to remain loving relatives—to keep a good sense of one's healthy separateness as well as one's concerns. Somewhere in that balance is the reasonably satisfying combination of responses that allows cousins and in-laws to love each other as well as themselves.

There is no way to overestimate the strength and support that come from knowing that responsive relatives and friends are never very far off. That does not, however, mean that they have to live next door or be present on all occasions. People stay on good terms when they learn the secret of respecting each other's individuality and when they do not keep crowding into each other's life-space insensitively. An individual family needs to share things with other members of the clan but it must remain—and fight for it if necessary—separate in identity and spirit if it is going to be healthy. Not only should social relationships show some sense of restraint, but other activities should reflect this wisdom as well. For example, it is a real test of a family to have in-laws or cousins—or sometimes even brothers—in the same business together. Dissension over money, its management and its investment, has made a great many people settle for less than the happiness they deserve in life. Intermingling one's finances is almost as dangerous as telling relatives how to raise their children, adjust their marriages, or take care of their pets. Nothing keeps a family on better terms than a little distance; that has to be psychological but it may be abetted if the distance is physical as well.

As people come to middle age they begin to wonder whether the stress of life will ever taper off. They find, in a good many cases, however, that life's midpoint is an unexpected focus of stresses from both sides of the genealogical continuum. Just as a mother or father may feel they are practically through raising their children they find that they have the new responsibilities toward their aging and sometimes ill parents. Sooner or later this problem of family living touches everyone; for some it becomes a major burden.

Circumstances vary so much that it is difficult to generalize about the response individuals should make to parents who are ill, aged, or otherwise in need of their emotional support. How to do the right thing is the hard thing; how, in other words, to manage this responsibility without having it overshadow or completely dominate their own family life. It is a long term stress and, as with all stresses, some anticipation, planning and cooperation among family members is necessary. This is true even if there are only two people involved together in sharing the responsibility. Working out their feelings about the task and accepting the challenge together will surely make it easier to manage in reality.

Anticipation and openness are important because taking care of one's parents can reactivate conflicts or problems which have lain sleeping in the person's unconscious for a long time. It is a significant life experience and something happens to us as we take it on. We can grow—and even help older people meet the real developmental challenges of growing old—or we can collapse under the weight of unidentified emotions. The chief one of these is guilt, an unhealthy source of motivation for taking care of anybody. Guilt abounds in these situations, however, and can be very destructive if it is left unanalyzed or unattended. The persons who are committed to caring for their parents should try to understand exactly what they feel about the situation. They won't die if they discover that they have mixed emotions; they will, in fact, live with the challenge much better if they identify their real experiences accurately. These mixed feelings lose their manipulative force when we can name and accept them as part of our humanity.

Taking care of older people may bring out the *Joan of Arc* syndrome in some persons. This is a martyr-like willingness to take care of everything for older parents, even when they are quite able to take care of many things quite well for themselves. When this complex surfaces, it is frequently a response to the children's unresolved feelings rather than to the parents' true needs. The balance of dependence and independence is every bit as important in dealing with the older generation as it is with the younger. Living with this aspect of family life means, as it does with all other aspects of it, working it out steadily and calmly as it manifests itself. It requires a deep and calm kind of love that works because it neither deceives nor overdramatizes itself.

In the long run, common sense, reasonable openness to growth, and a sense that a little of the right kind of love makes up for a lot of other things that we may do wrong; these can aid us in understanding the religious nature of family life and help us to respond to it with the faith which, despite our jumbled faults, has the power to make us, and those we love, whole.

CHAPTER FIVE

Living With Stress

Stress follows us through life like a shadow and it does not disappear merely because we look away from it. In a curious way, stress resembles other experiences, like happiness, that are familiar but difficult to define. This is because they are by-products of engaged living; we only know them if we say *yes* to our existence and its challenges. Stress goes with purposeful activity the way mist rises from a swiftly running river or clouds of dust swirl above an army marching across the desert. It is stressful to be alive, to love, to be disappointed, to meet deadlines, and to do any of the countless other things that make up the substance of our inhabiting the human situation.

One of the signs of psychological health is a good capacity to handle the inevitable stress of life. This consists of a well-developed set of internal and external responses, some of which are not entirely conscious to us, and which the experts have christened as *coping mechanisms*. A good coping mechanism, for example, consists in being able to reflect on the changes that take place in our emotions during the course of a busy day. When we can acknowledge them, even when this is somewhat painful or embarrassing to do, we make smooth the grinding wheel of stress. When we deny or distort our experiences, instead of facing into them, we become accomplices in wearing down our own psychological strength. Not admitting the truth about our feelings is, in other words, an ultimately ineffective coping mechanism. The trouble for most of us comes when, because of an accumulation of stress or because of its overwhelming character, our own healthy coping devices, like telephone lines under heavy snow, sag and finally collapse on us. We need to look closely at this possibility because, no matter how healthy we are, it can happen to any of us. There are things to learn about stress if we are going to live successfully with it.

Stress itself is a complicated phenomenon. It is not all bad and, in fact, a certain amount of it is actually essential for sound personal functioning. You cannot get through life—or for that matter, be very human—by being freaked out against the ravages of the human condition. Stress pulls us together and enables us to respond to our environment, to take up its challenges, and to make something of ourselves. Stress is not some Horatio Alger, Protestant-ethic device, however, which we invoke to insure hard work and final success. As far back as we can look we recognize it as part of human affairs and note observers and thinkers who have commented on it as an important factor in living. An element of stress is always involved with growth, for example, and an expenditure of stress is always required in writing a poem, painting a picture, or in doing any kind of worthwhile thing. We respond creatively, in other words, to a proper amount of stress; it is the overload that gets us down. And it is maintaining the balance that gets us through.

Man always seeks to get himself back into balance, even at the biological level where, through the process known as homeostasis, he maintains the levels of the biochemical elements in the body. He maintains a constant temperature, for example, despite wide variations in the temperature of the external environment. There is a certain amount of responsive striving required to readjust to the shifting stresses around us; that is what is going on all the time both psychologically and physically in each of us. As the famous researcher of·stress, Dr. Hans Selye, has pointed out, the experience of stress mobilizes us to respond positively to life. Evidence of this is piled up in the corridors of history, even in the instinctive and nonscientific efforts to cure people of various diseases by subjecting them to some kind of controlled stress. Bloodletting, shock treatments, and other forms of bodily and emotional confrontation have been employed to muster the personal defenses of the individual. As the ancient Greek physician Hippocrates noted, the experience of disease is never totally passive. There is the aspect of suffering (the *pathos* in Greek) but there is also the aspect of response, the work or toil involved in being sick (the *ponos*). Nobody would ever get better, in other words, except for this extraordinary human capacity to regroup the forces of health and to send them into struggle with the stressful forces of illness. Life in general may be thought of in accord with this model; we interact with the stresses of life, discovering and refining our own strengths in the process, and becoming more of ourselves as we search within for the energies to make and continually remake ourselves. Dealing with stress, then, and learning to live constructively with it constitute large segments of the business of life.

What about this regular if uninvited guest at our table? What do we know of its essential identity? In truth, stress, like the wind, is better known in its effects than in itself. We approach it in terms of its sources and the nature of the stress which they generate. One could trace an arc of stresses, descending from those major disruptive events that occur seldom but with great impact to those lesser phenomena which occur fairly regularly but less dramatically. Psychiatrists have provided us with a term to describe what happens to us when, anywhere along this arc, the coping mechanisms which we ordinarily employ to deal with stress break down in some way or other—we are constantly vulnerable to *transient situational disturbances.* These are something like the measles; most of us have them at one time or another. Transient situational disturbances are, in other words, the inheritance of the ordinary person whose ability to cope may falter under the pile-up of life's pressures.

There are, first of all, gross stress reactions that are associated with major interferences in our ordinary life pattern. We are subject to this, for example, if we are suddenly caught up in a disaster such as an earthquake, a bombing, or a flood. Major stress is also associated with a serious illness or an accident in which we are threatened with great loss of self-esteem or self-confidence. Everybody knows that stress is involved in events of this kind but few people are prepared to react effectively when disaster or illness do come into their lives. Most people can't even find the first aid kit when they have a cut finger. Research has shown that the *unexpectedness* and *unfamiliarity* of these experiences can disorient an individual and not only rob him or her of the capacity to respond but also evoke peculiar or bizarre behaviors. Gross stress is also aggravated if the precipitating difficulty is prolonged or if there is no effective way to respond to or escape from it. Separation from the person or persons on whom we ordinarily depend for support is also a factor in multiplying the effects of major stress.

Ordinarily a seriously stressful incident arouses fear and this moves us to the "fight or flight" reaction. We either get organized to escape the scene or we pull ourselves together to react constructively, to fight in some way. The overwhelming nature of some disasters finds certain persons incapable of doing either; instead, they move about aimlessly, or head back toward the burning city, or engage in apparently random destructive behavior. These unusual reactions are not without significance, however, because in each instance they represent an effort on the part of the person to adapt to the problem. These are ineffective adaptations, to be sure, like the "staring" reaction that can be observed in groups that have just received shocking news such as that of the assassination of President Kennedy. Howsoever ineffective, and no matter from what levels of consciousness these behaviors spring, they still represent some primitive or tenuous effort to respond, to solve the problem of stress.

In major stresses, there are, of course, obvious things that must be done, from hospitalizing the sick to evacuating the homeless. What is important to note here is that, even though the immediately disruptive effects of the gross stress will improve with removal from the scene, traces of the experience may well perdure. These scars of major traumas may cause an individual to experience a variety of symptoms even long after the event that initiated them has come to an end. These include waking up at night or not being able to sleep well, nightmares, or other disturbances of normal functioning. These are the phenomena that we have to learn to live with for a long time after we have recovered from the illness or catastrophe which subjected us to overwhelming stress in the first place. These left-over emotional experiences subside on their own schedule; an ability to understand and accept these as relatively normal is of enormous importance in our process of readjustment to life. These effects are called *residuals*; that means they go on living with us—so we have no choice except to learn to live with them. What helps, besides being informed and philosophical about them?

It helps not to be a John Wayne freak who thinks that personhood is built on denying that anything ever hurts at all. It also helps if we can listen to ourselves and, during our period of upset, note some of the ways in which we try to handle these still quivering emotional reactions. Occasionally, persons develop other problems in their efforts to counter-attack or counterbalance these residual effects. A man may begin to drink more heavily, for example, or a person who never experienced sexual problems may find himself or herself involved in them. These are not difficulties in themselves; they only tell us that we are human and still under some measure of stress. To react by feeling ashamed or guilty may only complicate the problem and make the resolution of the stressful period more difficult. At times this is also the work of outsiders who, observing a change in someone's behavior, try to modify this behavior rather than understand it in the context of the original stress. I could make a long list of children, for example, who, in the name of doing good, misread the sudden drinking or other unusual behavior of their father after the death of their mother. The death of a spouse is significant stress and one should not be surprised to see consequent residual problems and perhaps some faulty efforts to cope with these. Instead of beginning to treat the father as a profligate, the children would be better advised to try to arrange the kind of help and support he needs to deal with the original experience of stress. That might require getting a combination of psychological and religious counseling, but it certainly does not include the ill-advised and panicky strategies that some children employ at these critical times.

Another lesson that can be learned from major experiences of stress is the helpfulness of anticipation and planning. This has proven to be an important factor in reducing the effects of stress in disasters and it has its place in ordinary life as well. When one can think out the possibilities of what might occur in a sudden emergency or if a serious

illness came into one's life, the event will be neither
so overwhelming nor so disruptive if and when it
does occur. Some people excuse themselves by saying that they do not want to think about unpleasant
possibilities, counting each day's worry enough in
itself. This, however, increases the chances of a
serious stress having a far more desolating effect
than it needs to have. Even to plan in general for
the unexpected takes the sharp edge off it, enabling
us to cope more confidently and effectively when it
comes. If we have been there before, even if this
is only imaginatively, the territory is not so forbid-
ding; we can find our way out more easily and without panic.

While this principle has primary application to
catastrophes, illnesses, and accidents, it can also be
applied to other personal emotional reactions. This
includes the realm of less dramatic stressful behavior
which, even with the best of luck and the kindest
of guardian angels, we cannot possibly avoid. And
this is precisely where most of the stress is for most
of us, in getting through the quite ordinary hazards
of everyday living. Take the problems at work, for
example, or those that crop up with job changes or
moving to another part of the city or the country.
The list could be extended to include the subtle

stresses of letting our children grow up or grow away from us, of watching oneself grow middle-aged, or of facing retirement. These are distinctive challenges and sometimes they play leapfrog with one another so that a person can be dizzied by the compounded stress that is thus produced. These situations can also leave their marks on our souls, residuals that arise when our unplanned response proves to be maladaptive.

For example, the person who does not have any idea of what to expect when the children finally leave home for good may discover a large and un-anticipated rent in the emotional fabric of life. Not until that moment does the man or woman face or admit how much having the kids around holds things together—and holds their marriage together as well. Part of the reason for the recent increase in separations and divorces on the part of older couples lies in the fact that they were unprepared for the stress of being alone together again. Getting divorced is an effort to deal with that stress after the fact. Some anticipation of the possible difficulties, some effort to think out and plan a new future, some work at re-examining and deepening their own weakened intimacy: these are the kinds of things that can make such a crucial difference in a couple's way of living constructively with the many stresses of their life together.

One of the ways we learn to live with stress is by learning to live with worry. Far from being something we want to stamp out or avoid, worry, as a form of mobilizing stress, can have a positive and constructive place in our lives.

The experience of worrying is not only acceptable but, properly understood, quite functional for all of us. Psychologist Irving Janis has used the phrase "the work of worrying" to explain this. This idea is patterned on Freud's insights into the meaning of grief and mourning in our lives.

Mourning, as he saw it and as we can also understand it, serves a profound and positive need in human beings. We need to grieve. The loss of someone close to us, for example, is never something that we can just shrug off; it reverberates in our personalities on levels well below our conscious awareness of pain. The concept of mourning, far from being sentimental, as some inhuman observers would have us believe, is vital for the reintegration of the lives of those who are left behind.

Mourning provides a period of time and the appropriate rituals through which we can "work through" the emotional loss we have sustained. There is, in other words, psychological work to be accomplished throughout the time of mourning—a set of experiences essential if the individual is to heal himself and feel whole again so that life can go on. Tears are not meaningless, nor are reminiscences about someone who has died; they are part of the work that we do in our times of grief. Persons who will not mourn or who feel that they cannot allow themselves the expressions of mourning only drive the problem under the surface of their souls; it reappears, as repressed matters often do, in disguised and desperately painful forms.

There is a native and intuitive wisdom in the sense some people have about their need to mourn. They understand, for example, that it cannot be hurried and they will tell you, "I'm really still mourning; I'm not finished yet." The same wisdom tells people when they have completed the work of mourning. I recall a priest friend of mine speaking of his dead sister whom he had loved deeply. "One day," he said, "I realized that I had mourned long enough, that it was time to put away all the pictures and mementos I had kept out for so long."

Worrying is just as functional and purposeful as mourning and it can be denied or forced out of our lives only at our own peril. Janis observes that worrying enables us to "work through" our fears in much the way we handle our griefs in mourning. The difference, of course, is that worrying provides us with a way of dealing with our emotional reactions *before* rather than *after* we experience some blow in our lives. Worrying, by its very nature, anticipates something that is going to happen; it alerts us to some forthcoming danger by sensitizing us to its early-warning signals. Each of us has this experience at some time or another; we sense what we might describe as a funny feeling about a situation, or we report some apprehension that we cannot fully explain. This is because at some level of our emotional functioning we are picking up clues that we cannot label accurately but which alert us to personally relevant developments. If we dismiss these signals out of hand we may miss something very important for our own safety or well-being.

The human person is made to notice things, even very small things—like a shift in the wind or a change in the tone of someone's voice—that translate into a healthy kind of worry response. Without this sensitive system—which is found in its highest form in artists and poets—we would not survive long and would soon be overwhelmed by sudden and unanticipated realities. This is why it would be

extremely dangerous ever to try to breed or condition the capacity for fear out of a person; we desperately need it to stay alive both psychologically and
physically.

Perhaps we can understand the work of worrying
by reflecting on some of the research that has demon-
strated its value in our lives. Only the very dumb or
insensitive experience no anxiety at all. That, of
course, may lead them to do what may appear to be
very courageous things. On the other hand, it may
also suggest that they just do not understand what
is happening inside themselves or in the world
around them. The genuinely brave person is the
individual who has some sense of the dangers ahead
and who prepares adequately to deal with them.
The courageous person understands what is going
on both inside and outside his or her personality;
in fact, their freedom to worry constitutes part of
their armament against being destroyed by the dangers or difficulties around them.

Research on the attitude of surgical patients is
instructive in this regard. Some people deny all
concern and seem almost unflappable up until the
moment of surgery; they are not going to worry
no matter what happens and they make little inquiry
into their own condition. A second group tends to

worry about everything in an excessive manner, driving relatives and the hospital staff to distraction in the process. Their worry mechanism is set at high, an adjustment that is as dangerous as no worry at all. A third group, however, experiences moderate concern and seeks a reasonable amount of information about what is going to happen and what they can expect in the way of discomfort after the surgery.

The members of the first group turn out to have a difficult time after their operation actually takes place. Not having worried and not having anticipated the difficulties of recovery, they are frequently quite upset and tend to get mad at the doctors and the staff for not warning them about what they were getting into. The extreme worriers are not much better off because they are so flooded with worry that they cannot use the preoperation period intelligently as a time to prepare themselves for the experience. The patients who experience moderate worry and who have some idea of what will happen to them come out of the situation in the best shape. They require only half as much in the way of sedation and recover in a more self-possessed and peaceful state. They have, in other words, accomplished the work of worrying in advance of their operations;

it has proved functional in preparing them for what they were getting into—and they get out of it better than the other groups of patients.

Aside from the conclusion which we have already suggested about the functional nature of worry, this and similar studies suggest a crucial variable that is involved in the important and anxiety-producing situations of life. This is the role information plays in helping people anticipate what is about to happen to them so that they can rehearse the incident mentally and thereby prepare themselves more adequately to handle it. Information is the most important of all the variables in the hospital study mentioned above; it seems to make the difference in helping people to work through and complete the work of worrying before the surgery actually takes place. The most potent combination is the freedom to worry in a moderate fashion over facts that give a realistic appraisal of what the individual will actually experience. The persons who deny anxiety and who do not want to find out what is going to happen are far more vulnerable to bad reactions on both a physical and psychological level afterwards. This insight has application, not only for physicians, but for all of us who have responsibilities for other individuals in any manner.

LIVING WITH
EVERYDAY PROBLEMS

Try to tell the truth: It is important that people know something about what they are to undergo, whether it is in connection with a family problem or a school exam. That gives them the raw material for healthy concern; the more it matches what actually happens the better they will get through it. Telling the truth does not, of course, mean telling horror stories that paralyze the reactive processes of others and make it impossible for them to do a little sensible worrying. We ought to tell as much of the truth as is necessary and do it as simply and unaffectedly as possible. Telling the truth does not include the "confrontation" techniques that are so popular among some psychological enthusiasts today; you are just trying to acquaint people with a realistic sense of what they are about to experience, not trying to rebuild their character.

Give people enough room to worry: The overprotective deny others the opportunity to face the truth of their own lives. This is a crippling thing to do to anyone and it is bound, in the long run, to have serious consequences for those deprived of the chance to experience constructive anxiety. Unfortunately, there is a great deal of overprotection in one form or another these days. Its common form is the "don't worry" approach but it shows up in many other guises as well. There is, for example, the "Keep cool, man" school of thought that cuts away a person's right to have upset and concerned feelings at all. A good way to wreck another's life is to convince him or her to deny his or her feelings in the name of a pseudo-adult stance of living above and beyond caring. This takes them out of the action altogether and makes them the prey of a life that can be very harsh and unforgiving when it finally catches up with them. The kids who live by coolness may one day react in the same way the unworried surgical patients did—with anger at those who failed to inform them about the nature of life.

Don't offer platitudes: Yet another way to prevent people from doing the worrying they need in order to survive and grow is the overpious and unrealistic appeal to religion. "God will provide," the preacher says as though the realities of the lives of people around him could be ignored altogether. That may be fine for the preacher but it is hell on his parishioners when they find that they cannot pay their bills because they have not taken the precautions that a little healthy worry might have inspired.

A variant of this approach, now currently enjoying a revival, is to face life by praying unrealistically about it. This does not just include the "deals" with

97

God that we tend to make when are are sick or otherwise pressed against the wall. This new-style prayer has far greater implications because of the subtle and perennial pull it exerts in turning people away from the sensible and concrete things they can do in order to make the world a better place for everybody. Praying excuses us from the healthy anxiety we should feel about the enormous problems around us to which conscience bids us to respond. Prayer all by itself has never been enough. Prayer works best when those who pray also let themselves worry about their contribution to the needs of mankind. That is why some courses of meditation to calm the soul may be depriving us, in the name of renewed piety, of the anxiety we should feel for all the work we have yet to accomplish. Here again, our anxiety should be moderate and informed so that we can reasonably take on those tasks which we can fulfill with our time and our talents. Faith never flies blind; it has a good sense of the world and it enables us to see it more clearly and to be concerned about it more appropriately. Mistaken prayer can lead many persons back to the exile from man in which prayer is just talking to ourselves so that we cannot hear the tremors of concern that should properly ripple across our psyches because of the numberless challenges of what seems to be a wicked and uninviting world.

Vocalize things to worry about: Lovers can also kid themselves about the signs that should cause them concern in their relationships. They sometimes do not permit themselves to worry until it is too late to do anything constructive about their long-simmering problems. Have you ever heard a man or woman say, "I never knew you felt this way about it!" or "Why didn't you tell me all this long ago?" When we do not want to give heed to the facts that should make us concerned enough to do something about them, we buy a little of what might well be termed "fool's time." Failing to read the signs, preferring not to experience the anxiety that is appropriate when something is out of phase in an intimate relationship—these give false and limited comfort to any man or woman; they are temporary and betraying strategies that may be regretted but not undone in the later wreckage of a marriage or a friendship. Worry, in appropriate amounts, tells us that something is wrong that only we can make right.

Sometimes the worries that we refuse to face during the day emerge at night to try to get their message across to us. They express themselves in dreams, but ordinarily these are difficult for us to analyze by ourselves. There are other moments, however, when worry nibbles at the edges of rest. We would be better off paying attention to these worries and trying to understand them rather than trying to drown them out.

These worries include the battalions that march across our pillows—even when we are very tired—the moment we turn off the light. These thoughts and images may have been standing in formation and ready to proceed all day. When we have kept them out of awareness by keeping busy or distracted, they seize the first moment to make their entrance. Their parading makes us restless but counting sheep or multiplying nightcaps will not make them go away. They are telling us of the worries that are at work on the underside of our consciousness. We would do better to try to sort these out so that we can at least be concerned in a constructive way about them.

When we wake up early and cannot get back to sleep, it is frequently a sign of the same kind of worry. There may be no armies of worrisome images, no definite shape to this anxiety, and yet it is clearly there. Perhaps an exploration of our current activities or relationships will reveal the cause of this situation. Waking up early tells us that something is bothering us at a deep level. It is as clear a signal as we are likely to get; its message is that we should inspect the rest of our lives more carefully.

We read in the gospels that Jesus told us not to fear; well, how do we square this with the idea that a little worry, like a little wine, is good for the human person? Jesus never asks us to do anything that is totally inhuman; he speaks always of those things which enable us to discover and realize a fullness of our real selves. He never means to rule out the work of worrying. Indeed, in the account of the agony in the garden, one can sense that, on the eve of his own death, Jesus anticipated and struggled through the reality of what lay before him. His was a realistic prayer, not that he be delivered from his anguish, but that he might face and accept the accusations, injustices, and sufferings that would mark the fullness of his work. Jesus did not fear excessively and run away or deny his experience; he looked straight at it, knowing a special loneliness that prepared him for the last lonely hours of his life. The tragedy is not that Jesus should have known fear in anticipation of his death but that he should have experienced it without the strength and support of his closest friends.

To face events realistically, to allow ourselves to

101

know enough truth about them, to become moderately and constructively concerned—these have never been easy human responses. They are, in fact, a part of the dying which we constantly experience when we are truly alive. The Christian senses a deeper mystery here, an understanding that even worry incorporates him somehow into the sufferings of Jesus. There is a profound asceticism involved in becoming aware of what is going on inside of ourselves and why. To do this a person must yield up preconceived notions, self-congratulatory stances, and the defenses that keep him from hearing the message of his own anxiety. He dies a little with each discovery of truth; what dies, however, are those elements of self-encapsulation which keep us from knowing a fuller and richer life. Resurrection is an experience that may be incomprehensible to the person who has never suffered the small deaths of ordinary living that attune us to the presence of authentic religious mystery in our lives. Even worrying helps us to recognize something of the pattern of life, death and resurrection which repeatedly recurs in our days as a sign of the ultimate meaning of everything we know and share together. Without anxiety, without the capacity to suffer and die and rise above it, we would never know who we are.

CHAPTER SIX

Living With Sexual Problems

Men and women go a long way toward living more comfortably with their sexual problems when they can live more easily with their sexuality itself. However one may expand the notion of a sexual problem, it is painfully clear that dealing openly and calmly with human sexuality has become a serious problem for a great many people. Human beings are still extraordinarily vulnerable in the area of sexual feelings and behavior; they can easily be intimidated or exploited by persons who pretend to a higher wisdom or a surer sense of how they should conduct themselves sexually. There are enough challenges connected with living a relatively normal life not to have any unnecessary ones superimposed in our experience, especially in a dimension of life that has proved to be enduringly sensitive. All the talk about sex in the supposed age of openness has seemed to do little to banish the anxiety and uncertainty which hover like wispy ghosts around human sexuality.

Words, in themselves, do not seem to be the answer. Sexual problems are not bought off by intellectual bargaining, no matter how fine the reasoning nor elaborate the information that is presented. Indeed, one is tempted to think that we have a surfeit of words on sexuality and that it is time to be silent for a while in order to give people a breathing space and some time for reflection. Everybody, however, has a plan for everybody else's sexuality at the present time; this reflects the agony of mankind's search for better self-understanding but it does not provide many solutions. Sexuality is, after all, a form of communication in itself, a language that may be hampered by too many translations. Perhaps it must emerge, find its own voice in people's lives, and speak ultimately for itself. One thing is clear: it will be a long time before the last word, much less everything you always wanted to know about sex, will be spoken. We may more appropriately begin with patience and compassion rather than urgent advice and judgment for all those who earnestly want to understand their own sexuality better.

In the long run, this less heated perspective may

be the most important first step for all of us in learning to deal with our own sexuality more constructively. The attitude of acceptance that we can bring
to our human inheritances is an enormous aid in
moving toward that fuller growth before which most
problems solve themselves. With sexuality the most
satisfactory solutions to problems may be the in-
direct rather than the direct ones. At the present
time, however, even the daily papers are filled with
prescriptions designed to improve sexual performance and satisfaction. There may be a measure of
good in some of the facts that are communicated this
way but the direct matching of specific solutions to
specific sexual complaints has disadvantages. The
most serious of these springs from the fact that this
view isolates sexual functioning from the overall
personality of the individual concerned. There has
already been enough of that in the history of the-
ology and science; one can say that many of our
lesser problems with sex flow from this distorting
overall attitude. In other words, sexuality that is
forced out of context by whatever combination of
influences is very difficult to reintegrate into personality. If, however, the focus is shifted to the total
person so that the attendant human values are more
easily seen, then sexuality becomes far less a diffi-

culty in itself because it is not isolated from the rest of human experience. The best thing for sexuality becomes, not some incidental and symptomatic solution, but the kinds of experiences that benefit the complete human being. What is good for men and women in general is good for everything about them, including their sexual lives.

This becomes more important as we listen carefully to individuals with what they perceive to be stressful sexual problems. Beneath most of their questions one senses a recurrent uneasiness. Although it is difficult for people to put these things into words—and many problems are presented as belonging to third parties—the unspoken refrain is often something like this: "Am I normal?" or "Am I like everyone else?" These are haunting questions for persons who may have had little if any help in understanding their sexual feelings and who have been instructed in rather absolutist dogmas about sexual adjustment. The cultural surroundings or other sources of information leave little room and provide little help to these people in understanding the sometimes broad range of feelings and fantasies which fills their experience. Add the fact that a distorted religious heritage may have made them feel guilty just for having sexual feelings, and a sense of their dismay becomes more evident and understandable. Many of the sexual problems of persons like these are present, not because of some inherent sexual confusion on their part, but because of the environment of sexual confusion to which they have been subjected. They need understanding and support to explore their own sexual uncertainties in order to gain the overall confidence in themselves which enables them to incorporate their sexuality as a healthy aspect of being human.

To that end, the best advice for most of us is to listen carefully to what is going on inside ourselves. Some people, hounded by harsh religious imperatives, believe that it is wrong even to pay attention, or to acknowledge, sexual thoughts. Better to turn these unbidden guests out into the darkness, they feel, lest they soon overrun the whole house. That kind of frenzy—that dreadful uneasiness about sexual feelings of any kind—causes a serious and harmful maladaptation to human sexuality. It encourages the use of defenses that obscure the possible meanings of sexual experience. A necessary preliminary to listening to our own sexuality may lie in coming to terms with these self-penalizing attitudes toward sexual feelings. That begins by recalling how much we constrict our view of life when we impose a limited number of constructs on it. For example, to look out at existence and feel that everything must immediately be judged in terms of whether it is sinful or not betrays an excessively intimidated view of God's good universe.

To assign everything to some theological enclosure of sin or virtue is to sharply reduce our possible sense of ourselves and, having thus placed ourselves on the chopping block, to spend the rest of our lives hacking ourselves to shreds. That approach is part of the problem rather than part of the solution. It makes it almost impossible, for example, to consider sexuality as an aspect of our biological and psychological development, as, in other words, a sound and healthy, if occasionally complicated, part of ourselves. The person who hurriedly rates himself as sinful when he or she is sexual automatically forces sexuality out of its fitting personal context. That makes a calm and unpanicked acceptance of burgeoning sexuality very difficult for ourselves and for all to whom we transmit the same attitude. People who go through life feeling embarrassed or ashamed of their bodies and their feelings make themselves exiles from the human condition. The challenge is not to give them a lot of soothing information about individual sexual actions but to try to welcome them back wholeheartedly to the human condition.

It is no small gift to ourselves to listen willingly and not to run scared at any of the human sounds that come from inside us. Perhaps we may need to be patient and forgiving with ourselves but, if we can manage this, we will be far more secure and untroubled by sexual confusions or challenges. A man or woman who is growing will meet and resolve these far more constructively than a person caught up in his own projected fears. Only as we sense our sexuality as a developing part of our whole selves do we even get a proper viewpoint on what sin really is. Much of the worry about sexual temptations has veiled our eyes from the concerns about man and his life in which questions of sinfulness more properly arise. It takes a fairly well grown person to be honest about his motives and intentions in the various actions of his life; it is not easy to admit the truth when we have used or failed someone else. It is worse when, out of idle fears, we have held back from expressing or experiencing our real selves in life. Real sins are related to the way we live and relate to the other persons in our lives; we cannot get a good look at that until we can accept and integrate our sexuality in a relaxed and forgiving manner.

Many of the incidental sexual difficulties of living

are related to developmental problems or are the echoes of unconscious experiences from earlier stages of our lives. We should neither be dismayed nor disappointed when such reverberations are felt in our persons or are unreeled across our imaginations. That is the kind of thing that will keep on happening into old age; some stray or unaccustomed thoughts or impulses may be the daily diet for the healthiest of individuals. Nobody, as we noted in an earlier chapter, is perfectly healthy and so we cannot expect an absolutely final and completely appropriate set of sexual feelings either. To track down the causes of these experiences is, for the average person, wearying and also unnecessary for their good functioning. It may be one of the incidental benefits of X-rated movies that nothing has been left to the imagination any more. This is not to recommend pornographic movies as much as it is to observe how, in their peculiarly regressive fashion, they may offer some reassurance to the common man or woman. Now that all kinds of bizarre fantasies have been projected on our movie screens as entertainment, average persons will feel less lonely and guilty because now they know that they are not the only ones who ever had such strange and disturbing visions. Man should never, in other words, be indicted because he is sexually stimulable in a surprising number of ways. Neither should we be intimidated by a world which obviously does not yet have an easy sense of sexuality. Some current openness merely reveals an emptiness in our culture.

We do not, however, need any crusades for or against anything connected with sex. Nothing has done more harm to human beings than ill-starred crusades, most of which are initiated by poorly adjusted people who want to use the crusade to ease their own torments. In the long run, we must rely on the good judgment of good people to set things right. Healthy people instinctively—and with none of the crusader's wild enthusiasm—sense what is healthy or unhealthy in their environment. They can tell the difference, for example, between a great artist trying to illumine man's pilgrimage and a grimy exploiter posing as an artist in order to manipulate money out of the gullible. It has always seemed to me that Jesus' words about letting the good and bad seed grow together have particular relevance here. The best thing we can do for humanity is to lead deeper and more purposeful lives, to widen around them the values that, because they are profoundly human, are extremely religious as well. Men and women need as much light as possible;

113

they have already had enough battles in the darkness around them.

There are specific, recurring difficulties related to the average person's experience of his own sexuality Living with sexual problems constructively begins by not being surprised or shocked by ourselves anymore. Our sexual reactions tell us something; we need to listen with understanding more than self-judgment or disgust. Most persons can handle the pattern of sexual responses to which they have grown accustomed; it is. when something changes or when something different occurs that they grow anxious. It may be helpful to realize that our sexual functioning can and does reflect our overall personal adjustment. Certain neurotics, for example, experience sexual difficulties as part of their overall syndrome. The focus needs to be widened to include the whole person if there is to be any improvement in the symptoms. People should, without thinking the world is ending, pay attention to such signals and, if they are persistent and cause anxiety, they should seek appropriate professional counseling. For most of the ordinary snags or uncertainties about sexual experience, just the freedom to speak about it to someone else is frequently enough to drive the demons away. A little help at the right time from a knowledgeable professional—rather than from a drinking buddy or the *Playboy* Advisor—can make a great deal of difference in an individual's or couple's happiness.

While there are many voices that tell us that things like masturbation, homosexuality, or having an affair are positive goods in contemporary life, anyone with respect for the complexities of human personality will hesitate to accept these judgments without question. There can, of course, be misuses of heterosexuality by the unfeeling and the selfish but this merely illustrates the need to inspect each situation in depth before passing judgment on it. To get beneath the surface of an experience in order to grasp its meaning is in no area of life more appropriate than in the sexual. The significance of sexual expression derives from the context of personality from which it springs. Sexuality simply cannot be severed from its human moorings or it becomes ultimately meaningless as well as bedevilling. We do not have to take a stern attitude toward the human person to recognize that fact. With what light we have, we must try to understand our sexual uncertainties, and, here again, we should get psychological assistance if it seems appropriate. Too many people live with sexual problems that continually irritate and embarrass them. They would live far more freely and self-acceptantly if they tried to penetrate these difficulties with understanding. Living with a sexual problem does not mean that we totally conquer or eliminate it; it means we have learned to deal with it without having it constantly deal with us. We may never finish dealing with sexual problems, but we won't live comfortably with them at all unless we are willing to begin the process. In many ways, that is the most important thing we can do: begin, with the right kind of help when necessary, to find what we are saying to and about ourselves in our sexual reactions and behavior.

Chief among the values and experiences with which we must deal if we are to promote growth in ourselves and others are the ones which center on what we mean to each other. Sexuality comes into clearest focus when, responding to someone outside of ourselves rather than just to our own needs or concerns, we break through the stifling layers of self-containment that so easily suffocate us. Many sexual problems are solved automatically as individuals improve their overall relationship with each other. Their sexuality then becomes a part of their life-wide pattern of sharing. From something vaguely alien or self-satisfying, sexuality becomes a less burdened dimension of loving. It means more as man and woman mean more to each other, as, in fact, they realize together the meaning of the reciprocal caring and tenderness that are the seals on our most fully human activities. We move, as Dr. William Masters has noted, from regarding sex as something we do *to* or *for* each other to an understanding of it as something we do *with* each other. When people are easy with that, they can live comfortably with the other challenges that life will steadily bring their way.